www.blue-way.net

Ulrich Golüke, born in 1952 in Neuwied, Germany is a systems dynamicist by training and has worked for the last twenty years extensively with scenarios. With others, he built up and ran for a number of years the Scenario Unit of the World Business Council for Sustainable Development. As a freelancer he has worked worldwide with companies, universities, foundations and students. He designs and delivers workshops and projects, gives speeches and writes. He is a visiting professor at the Business School of Lausanne where he teaches a course on scenario planning. He has lived in Wales, the United States, Norway, France, Germany and Switzerland.

Scenarios

How to Create them
and
Why you Should

Ulrich Golüke

Bibliografische Information der Deutschen Nationalbibliothek: Die Deutsche Nationalbibliothek verzeichnet
diese Publikation in der Deutschen Nationalbibliografie;
detaillierte bibliografische Daten sind im Internet über
http://dnb.dnb.de abrufbar.

Photocredits:
shutterstock.com ID 283173410
Lukiyanova Natalia / frenta

shutterstock.com ID 304776344
Makkuro GL

Herstellung und Verlag:
BoD – Books on Demand, Norderstedt

ISBN: 978-38423-4494-5

www.blue-way.net

Table of Contents

Introduction, Thanks and an Apology 7

Why bother? 9

The big picture 11

We matter 11
The future is wide open 12
The signal and the noise 12
Where scenarios fit in 15
Two development cycles 18
The Self and the World 19
The HOW in a nutshell 23
Scenarios are inductive work *23*
1. Driving question *24*
2. Interviews / Conversations *25*
3. Analysis of the interviews *25*
4. Two uncertainties *25*
5. Plotlines *26*
6. Causal stories with titles *26*
7. Application *27*
Scenarios are about people *28*

Phase 1 The Driving Question 29

Phase 2 Interviews / Conversations 31

Phase 3 Analysis of Interviews / Conversations . 39

Phase 4 Two Uncertainties 45

Workshop organization 45
Workshop tasks 48
Difficulties to be aware of I *51*
Rhythm of work 51
Difficulties to be aware of II *52*
Givens *55*
2nd task: Endpoints 55

Phase 5 Plotlines 59

Phase 6 Stories and Titles 63

Titles . . . . *.66*
Preview of phase 7 . . . . *.66*
Going home . . . . *.67*

Phase 7 Application 69

You enter the picture 71
Roman numeral I 73
Create a list of decisions . . . . *.73*
Draw the matrix . . . . *.74*
Fill in the matrix . . . . *.74*
Analyze the decisions . . . . *.76*
Roman numeral II 78
Roman numeral III 82
Roman numeral IV 84
Communicating 85
Next step 86

Epilogue
Scenarios are about people
and the Future 87

Appendix: Practicalities. 89

Core team 89
Writer . . . . *.90*
Growing the team, veto. . . . . *.90*
Be a mentor . . . . *.91*
Basic knowledge of the process . . . . . . *.91*
Starting a project . . . . *.92*
Scenario projects are like making a movie . . *.92*
What is a great facilitator? . . . . *.93*
Do you really need all these interviews, workshops
and core team people? 93
Confidentiality - a safe space for work 95
Cascade of Trust . . . . *.96*
Flow of energy 98
Difficult participant / team member 98
A Scenario **Process** is not Public. 101

INTRODUCTION, THANKS AND AN APOLOGY

I have been doing scenarios for about 20 years, starting with people from large corporations, then more with ordinary people and lately with teachers and students at the high school and university level. I have found that scenarios provide orientation in an increasingly uncertain world. They are one of the few tools I know of that successfully attempt the impossible, namely to bridge the gap between the choices we make today and the consequences we face tomorrow. They actually help you make better decisions today for an uncertain future tomorrow.

Scenarios are a tool for ordinary people to help them think the unthinkable, question the obvious and challenge the official future. They are a tool of freedom and empowerment in all walks of life, private, social, corporate and societal.

I learned that they particularly resonate with young people. The young have always created the future they need, and they will continue to do so. As I am getting older, I want to offer what I learned about scenarios as a powerful way to shape and transform the future to young people everywhere - and those who remain young at heart[1]. Maybe it makes their never ending task, namely to create a future in which it is possible for all people to live a life worth living, a little bit easier.

As Theodore Zeldin writes at the end of his book 'An Intimate History of Humanity': "History, with its endless procession of passers-by, most of whose encounters have been missed opportunities, has so far been largely a chronicle of ability gone to waste. But

[1] Martin, Eric Lee / Ross, Mark Stephen, „Young At Heart", Sony /ATV Music Publishing LLC, June's Tunes Ltd. Partnership

the next time two people meet, the results could be different. That is the origin of the anxiety, but also of hope, and hope is the origin of humanity."[2]

This book is the outcome of one of those meetings. Thirty young students met in the fall of 2015 in de Küper for a long weekend to learn about scenarios. I tend to talk and teach without notes, without powerpoint slides, and without visuals. Their feedback was that a few visuals and a few structured notes "would have helped". Well, here are both - and I hope they help.

A very special thanks goes to two of the participants of de Küper, without whom the weekend, and thus this book, never would have happened: Thank you Anne van Bruggen, thank you Jorinde Vernooij.

Finally, the apology. I am not a native English speaker and even though I love the language, it's rhythm and punch, I have never really mastered it's grammar, spelling and punctuation. Try to bear with me, even if reading the text is difficult at times.

2 Theodore Zeldin, 1994, *An Intimate History of Humanity*, pg 472, Sinclair-Stevenson, ISBN 978-0060926915

Why bother?

Any choice you make, any decision you take and any plan you set in motion will make sense or not, will turn out to have been wise or foolish and will be profitable or not, inevitably and exclusively, in the future. This being so you can, firstly, cross your fingers and hope for the best.

Second, you can rely on your intuition. Rely, in other words, that your gut feeling won't let you down. Many highly acclaimed leaders' claim to fame is that they have a superior intuition and without being able to explain fully why and how they decide what they decide, in the end, their decisions turn out to be right.

A third possibility is to ride a favorable trend. If things are going your way, if the rising tide, as we know it does, is already lifting all boats, it's probably difficult to make a wrong decision. But remember, in the end, the tide turns and a trend, as some of us have had the opportunity to learn, is a trend only until it bends.

A fourth alternative is currently much en vogue, namely to trust in big data. The hope is that some smart algorithm is going to save your day. But remember Nate Silver's admonition in his recent book "The Signal and the Noise"[3], who writes that the first, and sometimes only, thing big data does is to increase the level of the noise.

The fifth alternative, much liked by those in charge when things go wrong, is to delegate, and if all else fails, to deny responsibility.

---

3 Nate Silver (2015), *The Signal and the Noise*, Penguin Books, New York, ISBN 978-0143125082

Or, you could use scenarios to make better decisions today for an inevitably uncertain future. This short book is about the process of creating and applying scenarios in your world. About the *how*, in other words.

But first, let me write a few words about *why* scenarios are such a nifty little tool to have in your toolbox.

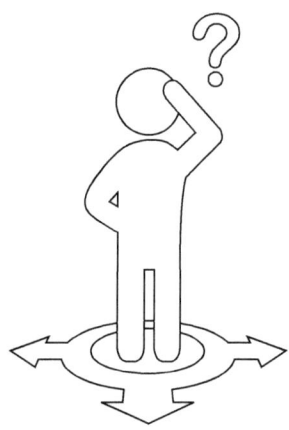

The big picture

We matter

Until a few hundred years ago anything we humans undertook did not matter on a geophysical, evolutionary scale. It mattered a lot to us humans, but the planet, nature and life itself just shrugged - if they noticed at all.

This has changed. Collectively, we now matter. We change the climate, we leave behind waste that needs to be kept separate from life for tens of thousands of years, we intervene in evolution, to name but a few areas where learning by trial and error won't work. Because the potential errors could wipe us out.

Still, we act as if there would always be enough survivors to observe our trials and draw conclusions from them so that next time we, at least, won't make the same error twice.

The power we have to change life, nature, the planet and everything in between will be with us from now on - you can't put the genie back in the bottle again. Pandora's box doesn't have a lid anymore.

So the very least we should do, in my mind, is to approach the future with a bit more humility, prudence, and modesty, rather than charge ahead without any thought, consideration or a plan B. Scenarios don't just give you that plan B, but also plan C and plan D.

The future is wide open

Until a few generations ago, what was to become of us was tightly prescribed by material constraints. If your father was a carpenter, it made an awful lot of sense to become one yourself. The task was to adapt as best as you could to very narrow and well-trodden paths into the future - and be content in doing so.

Today, already two billion, and growing, people in the world can be anything they want to be. A privilege of kings and queens in the past has become ubiquitous.

While we first thought that this was an unfettered reason for maximum joy and never ending happiness, we are slowly learning that this is also a curse. The freedom to choose becomes the obligation to choose. And coming out of a world of barely hanging in there, we are not so good at making choices. It is not in our bones.

Scenarios are a tool to put some order into the choosing you will have to do throughout your life. Rather than being paralyzed by all the options, all the opportunities, all the snake oil sellers peddling their potions, you can use scenarios to regain some control over your life, to live the story of *your* life, rather than the story someone else wants you to live.

The signal and the noise

Finally, a slightly more technical reason for becoming proficient with scenarios.

All data and information consist of signal components and noise components. And it's the signals that carry the useful bits we are after: news, facts, truth, reality, accuracy, precision and certainty. Unfortunately, they are buried, sometimes very deeply, in noise. Noise is distraction, commotion, disturbance and uncertainty. Note that I am using 'noise' here not as the intrinsic component of a signal[4], but the more colloquial background disturbances that smear the signal, all the way to totally hiding it.

So, what can we do when our signal gets lost in the noise? We can and must give it context. As Nate Silver writes "Information becomes knowledge only when it's placed in context." (Silver, 2015, pg 451) What scenarios are really good at is placing your signal, your data, into not one, but several divergent contexts.

Let's assume your signal is the word 'signal', written in black. If your noise is a very dark gray, the information content of your signal is very hard to pick out. Visually this looks like this:

Not easy to see, even if your eyes are as sharp as a hawk's eye. However, if you place the same signal into a different context, say a lighter gray, things become much easier.

---

4 … that the signal processing folks talk about - for a great introduction to this see Tom O'Harver, *A Pragmatic Introduction to Signal Processing*, 2015, http://terpconnect.umd.edu/~toh/spectrum/TOC.html, accessed Jan 2016

Signal

In the real world, the signal you are after is of course not the word 'signal', but a wild mixture of facts, ideas, rumors, disinformation, weak indications, of exactly what - you are not quite sure; all fuzzy, fraying at the edges, fading in and out and open to all kinds of measurement error and interpretation dilemmas. Just try to recall the 'signals' you had to deal with the last time you fell in love.

In such situations it is good to have a few divergent contexts at hand against which you can place your noisy signals and see if they become clearer.

Why do I keep talking about *divergent* rather than just plain old *different* contexts? Because I want to emphasize the fact that your contexts should really be going in vastly different directions and not just be slightly shifted instances of each other. With divergent scenario contexts at your disposal you see quite different things in the presence, and consequently, pay attention to. Or, as my mentor Betty Sue Flowers once put it more eloquently: "Your presence is shaped by the stories you tell about the future."

It is difficult to visualize this in a black and white book, but if, for example, your signal were a small mammal, then place it in a jungle, in a desert, on an ice float or the like rather than in a handful of slightly differently arranged ornamental English gardens.

Scenarios empower you and your team to actually *create* these contexts. In this little book you will learn step by step how to do this, and once they exist, how to apply them to your decision-making. As a result, the decisions that you take in the present will turn out to be better ones for the uncertainties of the future that will always confront you.

Where scenarios fit in

Like any tool, scenarios can be used improperly. The first check whether scenarios are appropriate or not is to ask yourself what kind of question do you want to answer compared to what kind of future. To my mind, the definitive advice was given in 1997 by Courtney, Kirkland and Viguerie in a Harvard Business Review article[5]. I will briefly summarize their advice.

Courtney et al. classify possible futures into four categories, according to their type of uncertainty:

- Clear enough future
- Alternate futures
- A range of futures
- True ambiguity

and illustrate the four with nifty sketches (my assumption is that their drawings are copyrighted, so you need to look at the original at the Harvard Business Review).

---

5 Courtney, Kirkland and Viguerie, 1997, *Strategy Under Uncertainty*, Harvard Business Review, Nov-Dec 1997 Issue, available here: https://hbr.org/1997/11/strategy-under-uncertainty, accessed Jan 2015

The first two, the top ones, are not, in their - and my - view candidates for scenarios. The future is too clear and too certain. The effort involved does not normally justify the added clarity, the 'reduction in noise', I talked about earlier.

The last two, however, are clear candidates for scenarios[6], since noisy uncertainty dominates the future. It is very hard to see the forest for the trees, to separate the wheat from the chafe. I would add that the third type of future is suited for working adaptively with scenarios while the fourth and last one is suited for working transformatively with scenarios. Adapting, shaping and transforming as they apply to scenarios is discussed in detail in phase 7, on page 69.

Another way to conclude whether scenarios are the right tool for your question and future is to look at the following sketch[7]. This one I did not steal lock, stock, and barrel, but in rudimentary form you can find it in van der Heijden[8], 1997, pg. 92.

Any choice you make, any decision you take and any plan you set in motion will be impacted by numerous factors or drivers. Very close into the future, many, if not most, will be certain and few, if any, will be uncertain (or noisy). Your certain-to-uncertain ratio is high. As you move further and further into the future, the ratio declines. The uncertainty grows, the certainty declines, and, in the end, your signal is swamped by noise.

---

6 There are other tools in addition to scenarios that Courtney et al. mention, go read the article.

7 All sketches, graphs and matrices can be downloaded in a larger size from www.blue-way.net/SceanriosTheGraphs.pdf

8 van der Heijden, Kees, 1997, *Scenarios: The Art of Strategic Conversation*, John Wiley & Sons, Chichester, ISBN 0471966398

In the beginning, there are many heuristics that allow you to deliver a decent forecast, including the old trusted standby that tomorrow will be much like today - and which is, surprisingly often, actually true.

At the far end, when uncertainty trumps certainty, there is only hope and despair. But don't dismiss this space too quickly. Because it is the space of imagination, of mystery and of new, often crazy

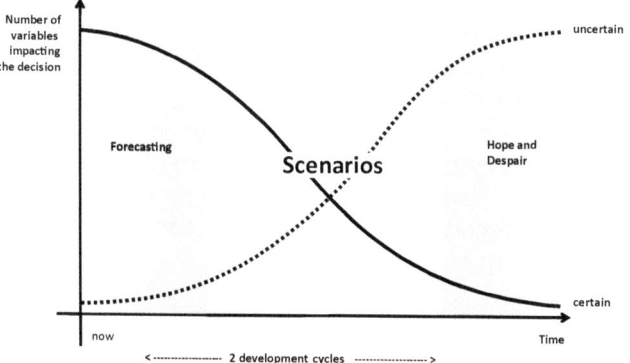

ideas - inspiration and creativity, in other words. On a more somber note, it is, as the great philosopher Karl Popper wrote in his "Logic of Scientific Discovery"[9] the source of the irrational element and creative intuition[10]. Dare to venture into it every once in a while, and come back to tell us what you found.

It is the middle part between forecasting on one hand and hope and despair on the other, where scenarios shine. The part where certainty fades into hazy <u>uncertain</u>ty, where what we know gives way to

9 Popper, Karl, 1959, *The Logic of Scientific Discovery*, Routledge, London, ISBN 0–415–27844–9
10 Popper, 1959, pg 8

the unknown, to fear and to apprehension. Where the noise at times is deafening. The normal response is to shy away, to retrace our steps to seemingly safe spaces, to familiar sights and smells and sounds.

We shouldn't. Instead, we should embrace the insecurity because life is deviation. However, just like a mountain climber is ill-advised to venture onto higher ground without the proper gear and attitude, we should embark on our expedition into the wild noise properly prepared and equipped. With divergent scenarios serving as our maps, we can deal with the uncertainty and the noise that are inevitably there. Through scenarios, we can turn them into manageable challenges and, on a good day, actually draw strength and energy from them. Scenarios turn future uncertainties into allies, rather than leave them as adversaries lurking in the dark, ready to trip you up at any moment.

> *"Alle haben irgendwie Angst vor der Zukunft, Szenarien sind ein Weg die Angst vor dem, was vor uns liegt, zu benennen und was dagegen zu tun."*
>
> *[Everybody is in some way afraid of the future, scenarios are one way to give a name to the fear and do something about it]*
>
> *A.O., High School Student*
> *Realschule Baesweiler*

Two development cycles

The time axis in the figure on page 17 is dynamic. It depends on the domain of your question. And to consider two development cycles is a purely pragmatic advice to husband your resources. If you are contemplating big changes - and scenarios deal with big risks and big opportunities - in the here and now, you need a lot of power. Because all stakes have been claimed, all deals been made, and all resources allocated. It is clear who the winners and who the losers are. But if you go out one development cycle, things are less cast in stone. Jostling for positions is still going on, and if you move cleverly, you can achieve big results with modest efforts.

Going out two such cycles, the cards are stacked even more in your favor. You can lay the groundwork starting now for the new world which you want to create or in which you want to succeed while most of the others are still celebrating the gains they made today. However, going even further out becomes more difficult again because you need to expend quite a bit of effort to make people focus that far into the future.

The actual length of the '2 development cycles' depends of course on the domain you are considering. For a software company 2 development cycles is a measured in months and maybe years. City planners ought to think in terms of decades and if you contemplate social changes, learn to think and act in generations.

The Self and the World

Having learned where scenarios fit in and when you should use them, they also give you an outside look at yourself. Even though this sounds a bit like pulling yourself up by your own bootstraps, it is much more mundane - yet still very powerful. Have a look at the following sketch.

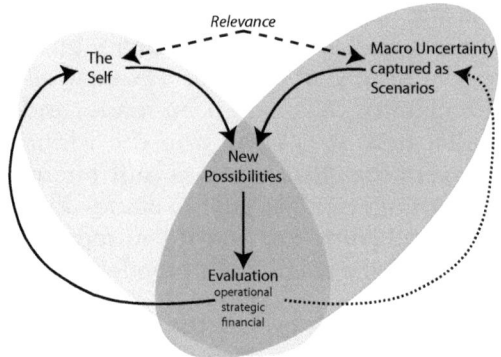

There are two cycles. On the left 'the self', 'new possibilities' and 'evaluation' form one cycle. On the right, 'macro uncertainties captured as scenarios', 'new possibilities' and 'evaluation' form the other one.

'The self' depends on the role you are taking on. It could be really your personal self; it could be your company - or some part of it, your group, your generation, your culture. Speaking about business, van der Heijden calls that the 'business idea', see chapter three in his book.

The 'relevance' in the sketch and the two dashed arrows leading away from it merely mean that the uncertainty and noise you consider in your scenarios need to be related, i.e. relevant, to the role of your chosen self.

The left cycle

Let us look at the left cycle. In order to learn, to change and to grow you think of, create and imagine new possibilities for the self in question. You then evaluate these possibilities according to their operational, strategic and financial constraints and, if possible, affect the self. If this last sentence sounds a bit too abstract, consider this example:

Assume the self is you. You wish (= new possibility) to become proficient in a new sport, say, ice climbing. You evaluate this possibility *financially* (can you afford the gear, the travel?, etc.), *operationally* (are you fit? do you have enough vacation? do you suffer from cold extremities?, etc.) and *strategically* (is your mate also an outdoor fan or rather a classical concert goer?, etc.) You find that all works out in your favor, so you do it. After becoming proficient in ice climbing you have, even if ever so slightly, changed - your new self is a little different from your old self.

So you can start again on this cycle: You wish (= new possibility), now that you are a good ice climber, to become an ice climbing guide ...

If this example is too personal, consider this: 'The self' is a group of loose friends studying the same topic, say industrial ecology. You wish to learn more about a subject not currently offered as part of the official curriculum. You contact an expert in the field and convince her to hold a 3-day workshop for your group. You evaluate this possibility *financially* (can you afford her honorarium? can you negotiate her fee down? etc.), *operationally* (can you all agree on a time? do you have a location? with food? etc.) and *strategically* (does this workshop help you in your studies, in your working life? etc.) You find that all works out in your favor, so you do it. After becoming proficient in the subject you have, even if ever so slightly, changed - your new self is a little different from your old self.

I leave it to you as an exercise to come up with corporate and societal examples.

The right cycle

This cycle overlaps the new possibilities and evaluation, but it replaces 'the self' with 'macro uncertainties captured as scenarios'. This is a clumsy code for the 'noisy, uncertain world outside'. And as we recall from a few pages back, the part of the future where certainty fades into hazy uncertainty, where what we know gives way to the unknown, to fear and to apprehension. Where the noise at times is deafening.

If we overcome our apprehension and turn the uncertainty into scenarios, we generate contexts that we can explore - well ahead of time.

What have we gained by doing this?

1) You have turned the key question about the future from "will it happen?", to "what can I do if it happens?" The first one condemns you to be a victim. You have abdicated the responsibility or control if something will happen or not to someone or something outside yourself. The second question, 'what can I do if it does happen', while not giving you complete and exclusive control, gets you to thinking about and preparing a variety of options you can execute if something happens or not in the future. And if that something ranges over a variety of divergent possibilities, your preparations can become more and more robust.

2) You are able to put the contexts you have created underneath the noisy, distorted and weak signals that reality usually consists of. By doing so, we are better able to recognize and pick out the signals that matter. They literally stand out. The result is that you are much less surprised as reality unfolds around you.

3) You are able to tell a convincing story. Rather than drown in the detail and minutia of life, you are able to see, live and stick to the strong lines of your existence. And if you choose to deviate from them for the sheer thrill of it, you do so consciously.

4) Finally, you have laid the ground work for asking an even more significant question about the future: "what do I need to do, in order to make my preferred future happen?" It is the question about transformations: "You see things; and you say, 'Why?' But I dream things that never were; and I say, 'Why not?'"[11] More on that in phase 7.

You see, scenarios are a nifty tool, and now we are going to learn to create and use them.

The HOW in a nutshell

Scenarios are inductive work

Since the future is not deterministic, the work must be an inductive process. Inductive, yes, but not without rules or methodology: To move from the particular to the general, to generate at least hypotheses, if not theories, the scenario process moves back and forth between stages of opening, i.e.

---

11 George B Shaw, *Back to Methuselah*, 1921, In the Beginning: B.C. 4004 (In the Garden of Eden)/Act I, § i

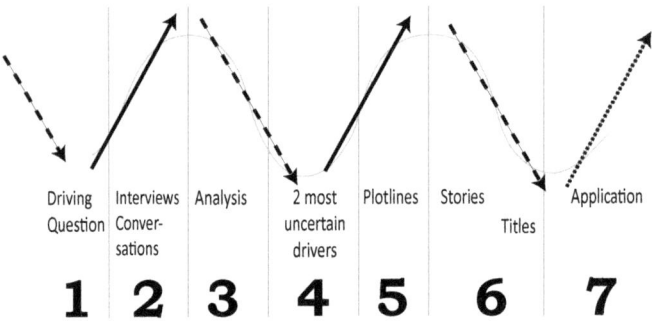

creativity (solid line) and phases of closure (dashed line). All this in preparation for the last phase of application (dotted line) - see chart above.

1. Driving question

The most important requirement for a good decision is a good question. So the time at the beginning of each explorative scenarios process should be used to make clear what you want to have actually answered by the end of the session. This driving question must:

– Be about the future (if you ask questions about the past or the present, you will spend a lot of time merely to identify irreconcilable differences, and you have no time left to shape the future)

– Be something that the participants can actually influence

– Be something the participants care deeply about

2. Interviews / Conversations

To prepare the scenarios, you interview 'remarkable people' about different aspects of the driving question. The interviews are open-ended and are more like conversations in which the interviewer speaks very little. The purpose is to bring the full range of concerns, views, hopes and fears of the interviewees with respect to the driving question to the fore.

3. Analysis of the interviews

All recordings are transcribed and the identity of each interviewee removed. Often the questions themselves are stripped out. Speaking from experience, one good way to do the analysis is to organize each answer as a paragraph and then sort the paragraphs in some form. Although this removes the flow and context of the interview, making it harder to read, it makes it easier to understand what the person said or meant. Each paragraph should be boiled down to one or two words on post-it notes. Eventually, these notes are clustered into themes.

4. Two uncertainties

The two drivers you need are those that are at the same time the most uncertain and the most important ones for the driving question of the scenario exercise.

There are two difficulties: 'most uncertain' and 'two'. Somehow we are conditioned to be highly suspicious of uncertainties; we seem to have to know – even if we have to fake it. Not to know is often considered a weakness. But the paradox is that to have any chance to ensure that what we do has an effect, we actually need to embrace uncertainty. If everything is already certain, then there is, quite literally, nothing you can do to make any difference at all!

Once that mental resistance is overcome, the next difficulty is 'two'. We resent, even fight having to commit ourselves to such a small number. Instead, we want options, choices, room to maneuver; ten, or more, action items and long lists of demands the other side must meet before we deign to consider their grievances! And so we have become 'list generators', forgetting that some things are more important than others; and also forgetting that having ten or more key points you have to act on – after all, they are key – you may be busy, but not necessarily effective.

5. Plotlines

The two uncertainties become the axis of the scenario space. Starting at the center of the axis, each of four small groups takes a quadrant and sketches a first story describing that future. They will then work all the way to the edge of the quadrant – i.e. throughout the entire time-space. The groups can either draw a path themselves or have the plenary group suggest one after a group has presented their initial story.

6. Causal stories with titles

The key to a good story is the switch from chronology to causality. In 99% of the cases, the first sketch created in the first workshop is a chronological sketch: A did this, then that happened, then C pushed B, D got elected, promoted or expelled, and finally F did that. The pattern is familiar because this is how we look at life and it is how history, overwhelmingly, gets taught. But chronology condemns you to be reactive. If time drives everything – as a chronological view presumes – then what can you do? Nothing at all – you can only wait. Instead, get participants to give you reasons and logic. Ask, like a pestering five-year-old, why, why, why? If pathways bend, ask what caused the path to go the way it did, and why not any possible other way? If most of the narrative takes place at the edge of a quadrant, ask 'how on earth did you get there from here?' If a deus-ex-machina appears, ask for the reason.

Once people think causally, get them to flesh out, repeatedly, the story with actors, events, dilemmas, the givens – all of them – titles and whatever else they can think of.

7. Application

This is why we do scenarios: to make better decisions in the here and now for an uncertain future! Scenarios give us a tableau of possible futures. So we now have three choices:

1   we *adapt* our strategies and (business) plans, at all levels, to the future landscape, so that we succeed by adapting better than others (remember, we humans made it thus far only because we are true masters of adaptation!)

2   we *shape* the landscape to play to our inherent strengths. The landscape of the future is not deterministic; it is full of uncertainties, surprises and chance.

3   we *transform* the future into what we think - with others - it *should* be.

The second and third routes are the real challenges. They require a keen and truthful understanding of one's strengths and weaknesses; it also requires a deep understanding of the room to maneuver one has; and it requires the ability to consider the set of decisions one takes as variable - more on that in phase 7.

Scenarios are about people

Paying attention to others, closely listening, putting yourself in the shoes of someone else, serving others - it probably is beginning to dawn on you that scenarios are for you if you really like and respect people. If you don't, perhaps you should get a job developing the next great algorithm.

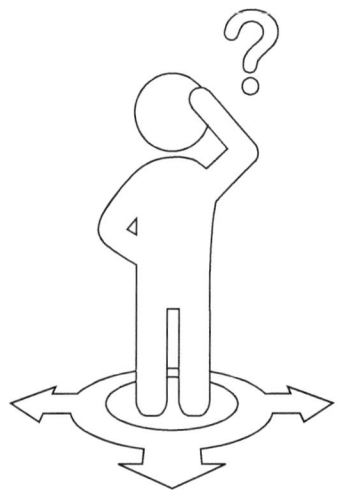

PHASE 1
THE DRIVING QUESTION

Driving
Question

1

If you don't know where you are going, all roads lead you astray. Also known as wandering in the dark. The point here is that when you consider a scenario exercise, be sure to spend a good amount of time pondering the question that the exercise is supposed to answer. Because if you don't, you are likely to squander a lot of time and energy and money and goodwill - of yourself and others.

Some points to consider:

- A good question is open-ended, and cannot be answered by 'yes' or 'no'.

- A good question is matched to the level of power and influence of the participants. You may not want school kids to ponder world peace. But should you happen to work with world leaders, you'd be amiss if you did not ask about world peace and human suffering. On a more mundane level, be very careful when you ask artists to develop a business strategy and hesitate to ask business people for advice on a play.

- A good question is about the future - should be 'no-brainer', but far too often we spend our precious time worrying about the past, and who the guilty one really is.

- A good question has a time horizon in it, explicit or implicit - so you land with your scenarios in the ‚two development cycle frame' I mentioned earlier.

- A good question has an actor in it, someone who causes something to happen, or not. It can be an individual, a group, a department, a function, or even humanity as a whole, again explicitly or implicitly.

- Beware of hidden agendas. I was once involved in a scenario exercise that wanted to ‚explore sustainability'. It was done by three dozen large, at the time, multinationals whose real concern was to explore if sustainability was a threat to their business model.

- Who decides the question? It depends: If you (and your core team[12]) do it alone, it is usually faster, but you may run into the problem that the participants do not view the question as relevant (enough). You then need to spend time and goodwill on convincing them, with arguments, not with threats and power. If on the other hand, you let the participants decide the question, you can be sure they think it to be relevant, but you may need a whole workshop to come to closure.

The driving question is the first time of closure. Because you select out of the realm of endless possibilities the one question you will use to drive the process. Choose wisely!

---

12 See ‚core team' under ‚practicalities' at the very end for details.

Phase 2
Interviews / Conversations

Interviews
Conver-
sations

2

In principle, interviews are simple: you use them to surface the hopes and fears, the dreams and concerns of remarkable people of the futures they consider relevant to the driving question. In practice they are difficult because of two traps we more often fall into than we are willing to admit:

- People are incredibly good at telling you what they think you want to hear, and

- you are incredibly good at only hearing what you want to hear and totally disregarding the rest.

What we euphemistically call 'conversation' is, in fact, 80% or more a one-way dump of information. If you don't believe me, watch any talk-show of your choice. And if you are skilled at observing yourself, observe yourself the next time you speak to your loved one about a difficult topic.

So this second phase of the scenario process is designed to avoid, or at least minimize, the two traps above.

- Select as your interview / conversation partners remarkable people. Remarkable people are those who can see things from different perspectives, can verbalize their thoughts clearly and can develop and communicate a line of causal reasoning far beyond the typical staying on the surface. They are able to self-reflect.

- Remarkable people are rarely experts in their field. Experts are experts because they have become very knowledgeable about ever narrower areas of knowledge and information.

- Talk to people from a wide variety of backgrounds. The more diverse your pool, the better.

- Do not forget to talk to young people. They, contrary to many others, will actually live in the futures you explore.

- Talk to three dozen or more. Once the number of conversation exceeds, say, a hundred, the additional insights you gain begin to diminish. For political reasons, it may, however, be necessary to include more so that nobody feels left out and that all the voices are heard.

- The conversations are confidential to all third parties, including those who pay for the project. This means that you may *only* reveal who it is that you talk to, but you may never ever quote or publish anything they said to you. Make sure at the beginning of the interview that this is understood and accepted by the person you are about to talk to.

- Despite the fact that the conversations are confidential, you should get the interviewees permission to record what is being said. This is an effective way of guarding against trap # 2, namely that you only hear what you want to hear. If you do not get the permission, *then you do not record the conversation.* Thus, you need to take good notes if this happens during the interview. Immediately after the interview, take enough time to write down your fresh, direct and unfiltered impressions.

- Interviews are one-on-one and take place in a location the interviewee chooses. Normally, this is their office. The only exception to the one-on-one rule is if you know in advance that you are not allowed to record the conversation. Then it is admissible to bring a colleague from the core team with you whose exclusive role it is to take notes. This should be communicated to the interviewee in advance.

- Interviews last for about an hour and should only in truly exceptional situations reach or exceed two hours.

- The questions themselves are open-ended and designed to surface the hopes and dreams, fears and concerns of the person you're talking to, with respect to the driving question of the scenario process. As interviewer, you need to listen carefully and follow the lead the interviewee provides in his or her responses to your prompts. Speak very little yourself, and listen carefully.

- A good way to start the conversation is with a dissonance between hearing and seeing. For example, if you are involved in a scenario project that explores sustainability, you could ask: „If you hear the word ‚sustainability' what images emerge in front of your mind's eye?"

- Additional questions to keep the conversation going are to ask, for example:

  — What is a good future?

— What is a bad future?

— Who do you believe controls or influences the way your future will unfold?

— Do you feel comfortable that these people, structures, organizations influence your future? Do you trust them?

— What are the two or three things you need to do right away so that the future will be a favorable one to you?

— How do you explain to your children, your nieces, young people in general what it is that you do? 20 - 30 years from now, will your answer be different?

— What is the relevant time horizon for considering these issues?

— What time horizon do you use in your professional work? In your daily life?

— What blocks social innovation and change? What encourages it?

— Is your company / organization trusted? Why? Why not? How do you know?

— When your task is done and it is time to go, what do want your colleagues / your friends to say about you? What do want to leave behind?

— Is there anything you've been waiting to say, but the right question never came?

Finally, use your own curiosity to add your own questions!

The overriding advice beyond any specific questions is to try to enter their world, as a guest, I want to stress, and try to see things from their point of view. Walk a mile in their shoes, if they let you.[13]

- At the *start* of the interview, you should give your interviewee a brief overview of the project, the driving question, who sponsors and pays for this, the role of interviews in the process, what will happen to the information you gather from him or her, when the final results will be available, who gets to see them and if he or she would like to be kept in the loop. You should also discuss and agree on the confidentiality of the interview.

- At the *end*, you obviously thank them for their time and their willingness to explore possibilities of the future, which may be quite distinct from the official future of the organization in question. More importantly, you tell them in a succinct way what happens to the thoughts and ideas they *have entrusted to you*, because an absolutely critical part of any scenario process is the transfer of trust: from the interviewees to the workshop participants, from the workshop participants to the writer / editor and from the writer / editor to the decision makers. If this flow is not working, the end product, better decisions in the presence, is compromised. You are responsible for that flow![14]

- If interviewees have additional questions about what happens next, their role, the overall process, etc. you should answer them briefly and

13 To me, Joe South put it best in his song, *Walk a mile in my shoes* http://www.metrolyrics.com/walk-a-mile-in-my-shoes-lyrics-joe-south.html
14 There is more detail about this ‚flow of trust‘ at the end under ‚practicalities‘.

truthfully. You may also at this stage ask them if they would recommend additional remarkable people that you ought to talk to.

- Finally, if in your judgment this person would be a suitable candidate for one of the following workshops, you should briefly discuss with him or her if their participation is something they might be interested in. You should not on the spot promise them that they can attend, this is a decision that you can only take in consultation with your entire core team.

- Finally, here are seven tips for empathetic listening[15]:

  — Pay attention to the body language of the person you talk to

  — Pay attention to *your own* body language

  — Avoid distraction. Turn your phone off!

  — Ask questions that deepen what the other person is trying to say

  — Don't insist on your thoughts, statements, ideas being right

  — Paraphrase what you are told, so the interviewee has the chance to correct, elaborate, expand what he or she is trying to tell you

  — Wait a few seconds when your interviewee has finished a thought before you speak. That gives him or her the chance add something crucial that otherwise might have remained unspoken.

---

15 Paraphrased from an article in *Die Zeit*, Specht C. and Penland PR, *Wer etwas zu sagen hat, muss zuhören können*, Zeit Online http://www.zeit.de/karriere/2016-02/aktives-zuhoeren-kommunikation-verbesserung accessed Feb 1016

Interviews are the first opening phase of a scenario process. Guided by the driving question, you let the people you talk to expand your horizon in all directions and across all levels. It is dizzying at times but stay with the thrill. Ordinary people become remarkable when given half a chance. Savor the energy they give you.

Phase 3
Analysis of Interviews / Conversations

Analysis

3

After the exhilaration of the opening interviews comes the closure of their analysis. Why not stay with the buzz, you may ask yourself. Because without repeated closure, you end up with so many ideas, so many directions and so many possibilities, that you are paralyzed into numb inaction. I am sure you all have had the experience of these wonderful brainstorming sessions where the post-its flourish, the flip-charts[16] get filled, the walls are covered knee-deep in brilliant, and not quite so brilliant, thoughts, the lead facilitator, or his or her helper, just before they fly home or, more likely, to their next critical engagement with one of the leading global players, take pictures of all the writing on the wall - and then --- nothing.

We are good at brainstorming, at generating lists of 10, 20, 50 key actionable items that all need to be worked on immediately if not sooner. But we are not so good at deciding on the two, three really important things that make up life, out of the ocean of possibilities. However, not to take that step of closure is a sure way to get to nowhere, since your energy, time and resources are spread over too many things that need attending, ensuring that in the end none of them get the attention to make a difference. While *you* are exhausted, nothing will have changed.

---

16 or their cloud-based electric equivalents

So, take a deep breath and embrace closure!

The three tasks of this phase are to hear what the interviewees actually told you, to summarize the messages and to prepare a presentation of them for the workshop.

Let me start with the hearing. There are *three kinds of listening*. I'll go through them in decreasing order of frequency. The first is where you don't actually care what the other person says, you tap your feet, wiggle in your seat, look out the window, check your smartphone and can't wait for the other person to finally finish so *you* can say what needs to be said.

The second kind of listening is when you do pay attention to what the other person is saying, but only in order to find the hook for your counter argument that destroys your opponent's reasoning.

Needless to say, it is the third kind of listening you want, where you actually try to put yourself in the other person's mind-set to uncover what is important to him or her. This is sometimes called empathetic listening.

This is hard to do, simply because we do not do it often enough. Therefore, there are a few tricks of the trade:

- Do the analysis in the core team, away from the office, for two to three consecutive days.

- If you were able to record the interviews, have them *transcribed*. Costly but well worth it. Strip out the questions (i.e. everything you said in the interview) and reorder the resulting text by paragraphs so that the natural flow of the conversation is broken. This makes it much more difficult to read, but it forces you to pay very close attention to what was actually said.

- Distribute the texts randomly to your core team ahead of the meeting. They should summarize each paragraph, each thought on a post-it note. If you have a disciplined core team, they will actually do as told, but often they come to the meeting without having read anything, but with elaborate reasons for why they couldn't. In this case, you have no alternative but to set aside time for individual reading at the beginning.

- Second best, and much cheaper, is for your core team to listen to audio and summarize each paragraph, each thought on a post-it note. People should *not* listen to interviews they themselves did.

- Have core team members one by one step up to a very large white board (large sheets of brown paper pinned to the wall will also do) and have them place their Post-it notes in an order that they roughly explain while posting. Other members of the core team are allowed to ask questions, suggest different orderings and probe the presenter's connection between what was actually said and his or her shorthand noted on the Post-it.

- Once all the Post-its are on the board take a break and use 15 to 20 minutes to step up to the wall and have a look at the notes.

- The next step is to be seated again and ask whether any kind of structure around any kind of concept seems to emerge. This goes in the direction of the important and uncertain drivers which we will deal with in phase 4, but it is not restricted to two. On the contrary, you will most likely end up somewhere between seven and a dozen themes, drivers, or concepts which in the judgment of your core team best represents what the interviewees were trying to tell you.

- This is a qualitative as well as iterative process. The art is to find words to describe the themes, concepts and structure that encompass the hopes and dreams, fears and concerns of all the interviewees. The odd thing about this type of clustering, which is called inductive because it goes from the specific to the more general, is that you may end up with words and ideas that in the specific form you will be using them, were never ever actually said by anyone of the interviewees. You are after the spirit, the essence, the underlying facts and emotions of their contribution rather than an orthographically and grammatically correct quote.

- For those of you coming from the scientific, objective tradition this comes dangerously close to being far too arbitrary. The only way that I have found to guard against this very real danger is the integrity of your core team, both individually and as a group. Needless to say, your own integrity should not give any reason whatsoever to be questioned. Sounds tricky, and it is, but if you repeatedly and authentically remind yourself and the core team that your task is to *serve* the interviewees by surfacing their deep underlying fears and hopes, dreams and concerns, you're more than halfway there.

- Why does it take 2 to 3 days? Because you and your core team alternate many times between intensely focused attention to the text and complete letting go. Very few people can do this switch at the push of a button. Most of us need time for these switches, and even go outside, get some fresh air, go for a little walk, and sleep on it.

• Finally, the core team prepares a very light handed summary in the form of a presentation to the participants of the first workshop which happens in the next phase. Experience shows that a summary in the form of seven to twelve dilemmas works very well.

Why light-handed? Your core team's summary of what they heard should only be one of many inputs to the workshop. First and foremost is the participants own thoughts and ideas, concerns and hopes. If you make the presentation too slick it takes on the cloak of the TRUTH and participants hesitate, usually subconsciously, to voice alternatives to this ‚truth'. A light-handed presentation signals to the participants that they can and should both use and question, but above all, improve on it. On the other hand, giving no presentation is the equivalent of a completely blank sheet of paper, and you end up with a strong dose of ‚workshop block', a close relative of the well-known writer's block.

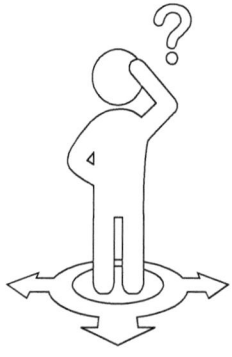

PHASE 4
TWO UNCERTAINTIES

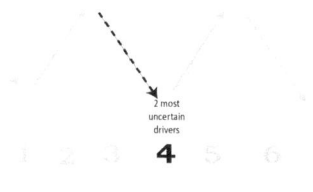

In this phase, you conclude the second closure phase and start the second opening phase. A difficult transition, because you do that in a workshop setting with about twenty four participants, plus or minus 3 to 5 people.

Why a workshop? You could, of course, do this yourself, or just with the core team. There are two reasons to go through with the cost and effort of a workshop: 1) You end up with better scenarios. Just as four eyes see more than two, working with a fresh group of people surfaces more faulty, shallow and flawed thinking. Better to find out at the beginning than when you have printed thousands of copies of your scenarios and are half way through the roll-out. 2) Scenarios are stories of the future and to have an impact, you need people to tell them. The workshop participants are thus your kernel of a group who will carry the scenario-stories to the world outside.

(If you do a personal scenario exercise, you, of course, do not invite two dozen strangers to work with you - although involving a few family members you trust is not too bad an idea.)

Workshop organization
- To start with the mundane, if at all possible organize your workshop as a residential three-day event. Being away from normal surroundings is

a great boost for the creativity of the participants and makes it easier to think the unthinkable, to question the obvious and to challenge the official future.

- You need a room large enough for all the participants and your team to do the plenary work in and you need four small breakout rooms. You can, if all else fails, use the large room for breakout work, but this is far from ideal.

- All the work rooms should have natural light, a flip chart or two and you should be allowed to pin papers on the wall.

- All the rooms should have natural light, windows you can open and look out over a bit of nature. Even a small garden, pond or field is much better than looking out over a six lane highway.

- You also need lots of post-it notes; they can be the run-of-the-mill variety, but they must be able to stick – I've had my fair share of struggling with Post-it notes whose glue simply didn't stick. While it is at times quite funny to watch your group's wisdom slowly float to the bottom of the room, in the end, it gets to be quite annoying. Hence, bring good, easy to use tape, just in case.

- You also need lots of thick markers. If you give participants normal pens or pencils, many will not be able to resist the temptation to squeeze in very small font long stories onto their Post-it notes.

- The breakout rooms should have one flip chart each with enough paper for the whole three days, and the plenary room should have two flip charts.

- *Visit* the place before so you know the people that run the location and, very important, have a look at their *food*. Make sure they can offer vegetarian and other dietary requirement choices. Buffet style lunch and dinner is organizationally preferable as well as usually cheaper than being served at the table.

- On the technical side, you need a beamer in the plenary that works with your laptop or tablet. You also need to be able to take pictures of the flip charts which participants will be generating in volume. It is tempting to use the ubiquitous smart phones to take the pictures, if you do so, make sure the resolution is good enough. Very often the resolution is set to work well for the occasional snap shot or selfie but is not good enough to give you the quality you need to be able to reproduce the pictures for the record of the workshop later on. Finally, in today's world where we are continuously online, be sure to organize free Wi-Fi. If this is not possible, make sure people know before they come to the location that they may be restrictions to being online.

- Prepare *name tags* for everyone. They should only consist of the first and last name of the person, and *not* include any title or function or indicate the company or organization that they represent. Remember, and remind everyone, that participants attend as ordinary human beings, *not* as representatives of something more or less important. The names should be big enough so they can be read from a distance. This is one of those tiny tricks that turns the attention to the individual and away from who they are or what they represent in the world outside the workshop.

Workshop tasks

On to the slightly less mundane. As the project manager, you are also the plenary facilitator, and you start the workshop with a very short theoretical overview of the scenario process. Very short means 30 minutes. It is not important that the participants get a deep and profound understanding of the process with all its detail, nuances, and elaborations, what they need to get is a feel for where they are in the process, what happened before and what will happen afterwards. Orientation, in other words.

You then moderate the introduction of both the participants and your core team to each other. With about 30 people in the room, that takes about an hour. Ask people also to reflect a little bit on why they're there, what their expectations may be for the workshop and if they have any kind of prior experience or exposure to scenario work, good or bad.

After that, you announce the ground rules for the workshop:

- Confidentiality, also known as 'Chatham House Rule'[17],

- empathetic listening, if this is new to you, read up on it under phase 3 above

- constructive criticism, which is criticism not to destroy the other's argument, but to help him or her improve - their logic, their wording, their pacing, their rhythm, etc.

---

17 „When a meeting, or part thereof, is held under the Chatham House Rule, participants are free to use the information received, but neither the identity nor the affiliation of the speaker(s), nor that of any other participant, may be revealed". - See more at: https://www.chathamhouse.org/about/chatham-house-rule/

And stick to them! (If you feel like it, you may write these rules - and any other you feel are important - on a big piece of paper and hang them in a prominent space for everyone to see.)

Then, one or two members of your core team give a 30 minute or so presentation of the analysis of the interviews. You then give the participants **their first task,** which is to spend an hour or two in small groups and come back to the plenary with **the two most important and most uncertain drivers of the future** with respect to the driving question of the project. The drivers need to be **independent** of each other.

They can use the input from the interviews, but stress that they are free to use any other idea, concept, driver, whatever that comes to their collective mind.

You need to have assigned participants to four different groups, something which I do beforehand by labeling the groups according to color, let's say blue, yellow, green and red and put a colored dot on their name tag, so they know which group they belong to. Your four small group facilitators in your core team will also have been assigned a color in advance.

Either you in the plenary or your small group facilitators should show the participants the template below. In the small group work, participants should step up to the board or flip-chart and paste their contribution where they see it in relation to

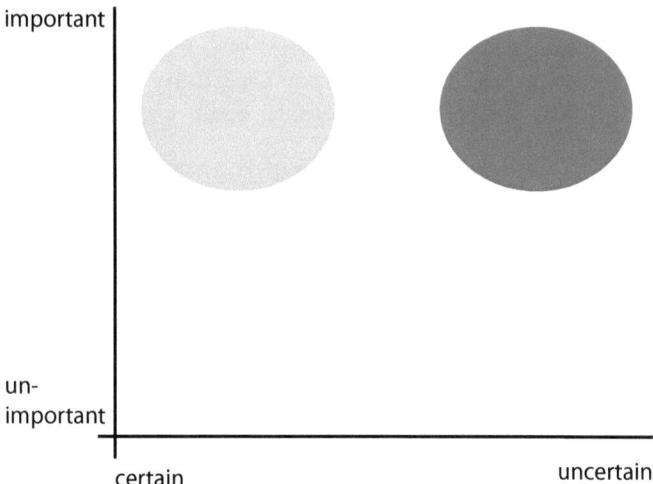

its importance and its uncertainty *in the future*[18]. If the group finds it difficult to order their drivers in two dimensions - importance and certainty - at the same time, have them do importance first and then certainty second. Takes a bit longer, but often helps people who have never had the opportunity to work this way.

When done, the two drivers they will report back to the plenary will come from the dark gray area. They should also note three to five drivers that ended up in the light gray area; these are the 'givens', highly important but very certain in the judgment of the group.

---

18 These are collective judgments of the small group about something that will inevitably happen in the future, and they may, with hindsight, be wrong. I remember many scenario exercises from 10 or more years ago where the prosperity and peace within Europe was a given - very important and very certain. Today, that judgment may well be different.

Difficulties to be aware of I

Two: We strongly, often subconsciously, resent having to commit ourselves to such a small number. We want options, choices, room to maneuver, ten, or more, action items and long lists of demands the other side must meet before we deign to consider their grievances! And so we have become 'list generators', forgetting in the process that some things *are* more important than others; and also forgetting that if you have ten or more key points that you have to act on – after all, they are key – you very well may be busy, but not necessarily effective.

Uncertain: Somehow we are conditioned to be highly suspicious of uncertainties, we seem to have to know – even if we have to fake it. Not to know is considered a weakness in many cultures. But the paradox is that to have any chance that what we do does have an effect, we actually need uncertainty. If everything is already certain, then there is, quite literally, nothing you can do to make any difference at all! You can wait and, yes, you can prepare for it, but you cannot change the course of events.

Rhythm of work

During the small group work, the plenary facilitator and the writer-editor wander from group to group (*after* the groups have settled into their work), listening but not saying a word –to get a sense of, a feel for the overall direction of participants' thinking.

After the work in small groups, participants reassemble in the plenary. One person from each group presents their findings while the others listen emphatically and criticize constructively. The plenary facilitator helps the entire group to agree on the two most important and uncertain drivers for their future. It may be necessary to go back and forth, because reaching two drivers is devilishly difficult. Often, more, many more drivers are offered and it is up to the facilitators to guide the group, large or small, to search for and find the deeper, more profound concepts that overarch the conflicting many, another instance of inductive clustering.

Reaching agreement on what the two most important and most uncertain drivers are, takes creativity, courage, trust, time and a little guidance. The guidance comes from the core team, the rest from the participants.

Workshops pick up the rhythm of the entire process: small groups generate, create, open up, the plenary brings closure - out, in - free associating, focus ...

Difficulties to be aware of II

What if small groups come up with 4, 6, 8 drivers?

Inductive clustering is the answer, i.e. the search in the plenary for words and ideas that in the specific form you will be using them, may never actually have been said by anyone of the small groups. Once again, you are after the spirit, the essence, the underlying facts and emotions of their contribution rather than an orthographically and grammatically correct quote.

Driver 2

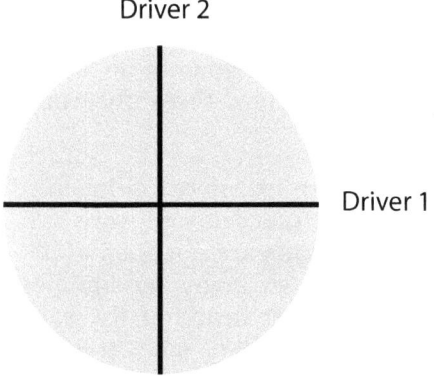

Driver 1

What if participants want a third axis in the plenary?

Sometimes participants may suggest a third driver, especially after you've told them that the drivers will be placed at right angles to each other to create the scenario space. Since we live in a three dimensional world, it seems silly not to use all three dimensions. Resist the temptation, for a very simple reason. If you place the drivers at right angles to each other, a space with four quadrants emerges - see above. Each of these quadrants be-

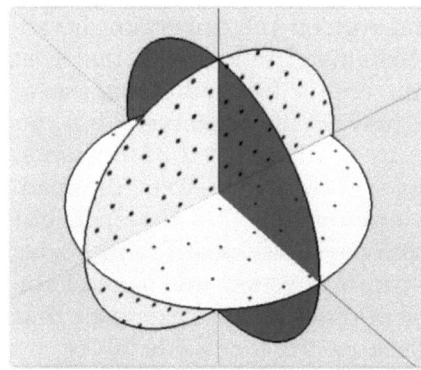

comes the home of one of the scenarios that will be created in phases 5 and 6. Each scenario will be bounded by two important uncertainties. So far, so good.

If, however, you allow a third driver, coming out of the flat space (like a z-axis), this creates a sphere, and you have eight spherical segments as homes for the scenarios, bounded each by three uncertainties[19]:

Not only does the picture get more complicated to draw, the resulting eight scenarios get very difficult to keep apart - we humans are not good at distinguishing clearly between so many possibilities. Let alone keep them all in our heads at the same time to be able to test your decisions (as you will do in phase 7). Hence, the restriction to two drivers of uncertainty is a practical limitation to increase the practical usefulness of your scenarios.

If nothing works

If the plenary goes on and on, if people fidget in their chairs, if the discomposure becomes palatable and the air in the room sticky, then the temptation to cut off debate and vote on the uncertain drivers may become overwhelming. The two with the most votes survive, and the rest is dropped. *Avoid this at almost any cost.* You may get the two drivers, but you also get your fair share of disgruntled participants, namely all the ones whose drivers were dropped. These participants may not rebel on the spot, but they are the ones who days, weeks or months later call the entire work into question and spread the word that this is one of those useless exercises that are doomed to fail because the method is faulty.

---

19 The SketchUp version is here: http://www.blue-way.net/ScenarioSphere.skp

Instead, try to get agreement on two drivers *as a working hypotheses*, to see, in other words, if they are strong enough to create, to craft a scenario space interesting, sturdy and powerful enough to support the creation of really good and divergent scenario stories. If they are, all is well, but if they are not, you must honor the promise of the working hypotheses and revisit the search for the two drivers later on in the process.

What if all small groups come up with same two drivers?

This is potentially more difficult than too many drivers, because there may be a perception that this has all been 'pre-cooked' and that this whole process is just a charade to lend an air of legitimacy to something that has already been decided elsewhere. Worse if this perception is there but not aired. To change that perception depends, in the end, on the personal integrity of the core team.

Givens

In the plenary, like in the small groups before, a list will emerge of the important and certain drivers. Keep track of them and also try to whittle them down to a few. This 'givens' must show up and be dealt with in every story that eventually emerges.

2nd task: Endpoints

The second task, first in small groups, then in the plenary, is to anchor the endpoints of the two most important uncertainties. The question that needs to be answered is 'How do I know that I am at one or the other endpoint of the uncertainty?'

This may sound odd at first, but it is necessary to ask, and to answer, this question because we all have different, often unspoken, ideas in our heads how to respond. Let's say, for example, that one driver is 'consumer demand', the task is to define the extreme ends of the uncertainty surrounding 'consumer demand' that the participants have in mind. An answer, from a real example I was part of, anchored one end as a world in which consumers were extremely self-centered: 'Me, myself and I' was the shorthand we used. While the other end was anchored by consumers who demanded respect for others. 'World-centered' was the shorthand chosen.

This discussion also reveals how far participants want to stretch the scenario space. In another workshop, an uncertain driver was 'sustainability'. Was the endpoint a Sunday speech about sustainability, the triple bottom line, the circular economy, or what? They settled on the as yet undefined 'quintuple bottom line' to signal that the end was far, far beyond what societies may consider when using the word 'sustainable'.

While the anchor, the definition, is rarely one that a natural scientist would feel comfortable with, it is important to get the groups to be as precise as possible. Natural language is and needs to be ambiguous, but it leads to the situation where different people hear the same word, nod agreement, but their underlying understanding is completely different. This leads to problems later on.

Sometimes it may be difficult to anchor the endpoints. Because it is genuinely difficult to do so, because there is an unspoken taboo to go very far, or because there is hesitation to speak the unspeakable. In such situations, what emerges as anchor points is often a shallow binary solution of 'good' and 'bad', or 'more' or 'less'. If you let these words stand, you are almost guaranteed later on in the process to have endless anecdotal discussions about what 'good' and 'bad' really mean. Much better to have stronger concepts and definitions to begin with. Remember and remind participants that the whole exercise is about the future and what may be taboo today needs to be aired tomorrow and the day after.

The endpoint discussion is also where you examine and agree on the time horizon. Having started with the two development cycles in the driving question, you get here confirmation on what to use.

The two most important uncertainties with their endpoints are the end of phase 4, but not of the workshop. That one goes on, ideally after a good night's sleep onto phase 5, the plotlines.

PHASE 5
PLOTLINES

Plotlines

5

The main reason to do phases 4 and 5 in one workshop is that even though repeated closure is crucial, it is not the most exhilarating part of any work, including scenarios. Hence, you do not want the participants to go home after wrestling all the possible drivers down to two; you want them to get the chance to experience what wonders the drivers are capable of bringing forth. Drivers are to scenarios what scaffolding is to a building - crucially important, but only there during construction - and often obstructing the view. Using this analogy, you want participants to go home from the first workshop with a feeling of all the new rooms' potential so that they get excited about the forthcoming move.

You start the day of creating plotlines with this sketch:

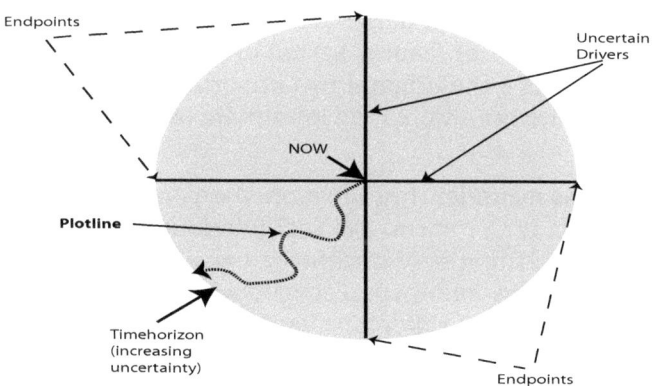

The uncertain drivers are drawn at right angles to each other, which they can be if they are independent of each other. The endpoints are defined and agreed. It is useful to refer to the discussion the day before.

'Now' is defined to be the center and the time horizon is at the outer edge of the of the scenario space. Note that as you move from the center to the edge, both time and uncertainty increase, recall the figure on the previous page.

The task now is for the four small groups to go each into one of the quadrants and in separate break-out rooms develop a plotline of a story from the 'now' to the edge of their quadrant. (Now it is clear why you need four small groups and four small group facilitators) This takes a couple of hours.

Then all participants reassemble in the plenary, present their story lines and pay attention to the three other groups' constructive criticism.

At this stage, there are several issues to be aware of:

- No story: If none of the quadrants come back with a story, or at least a kernel of one, chances are the axis – the original two important and uncertain drivers – were inadequate. Go back to square one.

- Paths meander through more than one quadrant: If this is the norm, again chances are that there is something wrong with the axis: sloppy definitions, very ambiguous concepts, not enough discrimination / difference between the two, etc. Go back to square one.

- Rotate & mix participants: You need to rotate the participants (and usually the facilitators too) through all quadrants. It is not any one story you want participants to be proud of, but the entire scenario space. Because that is where their future most likely will unfold. Rotate and mix groups, so they do not 'fall in love' with 'their' quadrant.

- Letting go: One very subtle issue usually emerges at that stage: Once we have agreed on the uncertainty of something, and the time over which it will play itself out, we tend to want to have something to say about this entire range. Putting people in one quadrant, i.e. restricting them to one quarter of the space in which their future will unfold, what you are doing is to ask them to trust others – some of whom may well be their sworn enemies – to create some portions of their possible future. There will be nervousness, suspicion, and hesitation. Respect and dissipate it!

- Timing: It is very difficult to know in advance how long people need for these steps up to here. However, do what you can to reach this far by the end of the first workshop, participants need some context in which their thoughts, discussions, and actions are placed until the next workshop.

The core team prepares a record of the workshop and sends it to participants one or two weeks after the end of the workshop.

PHASE 6
STORIES AND TITLES

In the second workshop, participants flesh out the story lines, invent titles, generate enough material for the writer and hand over the job of writing the stories to the writer.

- The second workshop happens about four to eight weeks after the first.

- About a quarter of the participants of the first should be present during the second. This ensures continuity of knowledge created and trust, and at the same time introduces fresh ideas, points of view and energy.

- For the workshop organization, check both under phase 5, the mundane bits.

- The rhythm of the workshop is like the first one: four small groups create and generate ideas, the plenary gives constructive criticism and feedback.

- Again, participants are cycled through the quadrants throughout the days of the workshop.

- There are *three* critical issues you need to handle well:

  — The stories must become causal. This is a big deal because most of our narratives are chronological, right down to our CV we craft when we apply for a job. A chronological perspective assigns to time the only power to act. Which may be nice for time, but not for you, since you can only sit and wait for time to unfold and hit you or not, or bestow happiness on you, or not.

It is a *causal* understanding that allows you to intervene in a system, to find and use the points of leverage and to shape things. How do you get to causal stories? Imagine a pestering five-year-old who ask why, why, why, why and why again. Get the participants, gently, diplomatically but compellingly to try to answer this imaginary five-year-old. Use turns, corners and twists in the participants' plot lines to ask why the story took this turn, rather than any other. Don't be satisfied with „Well, it just happened".

—   The stories must be stringent, novel, challenging and plausible. *Stringent* means internally consistent; there must be a causal (scc above) logic to them. To demand that stories are *novel* is a way to pull the participants into the future. We are incredibly influenced by the immediate past and present, so without your and your core team's continuously insistent prodding to move boldly into the future, you will end up with stories about things that are in the newspapers by the end of the month. A *challenging* story is one that is making the reader sit up and take notice, rather than put it on the pile of things to attend to ‚later on'. And finally, *plausible* means that the story needs to be grounded in today's world. It should and must leave today behind, but that is where it starts. Otherwise you are running a philosophical colloquium, which definitely has its place and value, but not when you are working on making better decisions today for the uncertainty of tomorrow.

— Actors vs. stage: Most of the stories you know and tell are carried by, revolve around characters, mostly human, and their ‚characteristics'. They are the ones that do something or not, are influenced by others, learn their lesson or not and face dilemmas, which at times are insurmountable - just recall Sisyphus. Scenarios, however, are also meant to be *used* as backgrounds for others, not involved in the creation of the stories, to improve their decision making.

To make it easier for these others to use the stories, they are asked to enter the scenario-story and evaluate their decisions as if the scenario-story, rather than their normal surrounding, was real. It is this ‚stepping into' that is made more difficult the more convincing the characters of your story are. Your characters are not just placeholders, they are there! So before others can ‚step-into', they need to get rid of the folks already populating the story. And if the story is carried by the characters, once you get rid of them - to be able yourself to ‚step-into' - the story may well collapse. Hence, it is better to create stories with as few characters as possible and to concentrate on the stage on which the story unfolds.

The workshop ends with three tasks, the invention of titles, a preview of phase 7, the application, and with help going home.

Titles

Titles are the handles with which you and the participants carry the stories into the world. At best, the titles carry within them the entire story - in reality this means that a good title evokes in the listener images very close to what the creators had in mind during creation. Getting to titles is the last time you use inductive clustering in the scenario process. Because chances are that none of the title words have been voiced during the work so far. So, set aside about three-quarters of an hour towards the end. Make sure the participants understand that these are suggestions, the final decision rests with the writer.

Preview of phase 7

The reason to do scenarios is to make better decisions *today* about an uncertain future *tomorrow*. The decision making is part of the 'self' I talked about on page 20 ff. Hence, it is usually not done in public and the number of people using the scenarios as their tableau against which they test, adjust and conceive their decisions far exceeds the number of participants. Still, like any parent, participants are quite interested in what happens to their offspring and so you should give them an overview of phase 7 (see below). You should also invite participants to consider becoming themselves users of the scenario and organize well-defined groups who want to increase the signal and lower the noise in their worlds, i.e. make better decisions.

Going home

Scenario creation is an unusually engaging and mind-opening experience. Ordinary people gather to think about the unthinkable, to question the obvious and to challenge the official future. All in a setting of trust and creativity. Something we are rarely called upon and rarely experience in our daily lives. And what is more, they actually, with the help of the core team, deliver. Hence, a special group feeling emerges that is often quite at odds with what expects us back at work on Monday morning.

The *first* step in helping participants bridge this gap is to talk about it. Not at great length, but enough to signal to the group that you are aware of it and that it is normal. The *second* step is to offer them a presentation of the scenarios in their company or organization. The presentation should be done by one of the core team, not a workshop participant who may well be a competitor. The *third* step is to offer to run an application workshop for them.

Finally, the core team prepares again a record of the workshop and sends it to participants one or two weeks after the end of the workshop. Additionally, the core team manages the writing and communication between writer and participants.

If your budget permits, create a half day event where you release the scenario stories to the public in a proper media event. Make sure the participants are invited to this event and receive the final stories ahead of time.

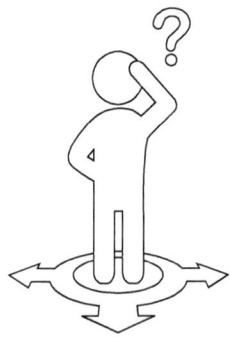

PHASE 7
APPLICATION

This phase is *why* we do scenarios. To use them as a sounding board **7** for our decisions[20], either to adapt to possible futures or to try to shape or transform the future to come. It is also where the public part of the work becomes private, especially if you do scenarios with or for corporations.

Applying scenarios is tricky for three reasons:

1 Testing your decisions against a tableau of possible futures is the basis for the strategy of your organization, your business and/or your own life. Hence, it is the essence of what you are about, which, by nature, is often private and thus rarely talked or written about.

2 If you were part of creating the scenarios, you need to *radically* shift perspective: While creating scenarios, the future is wide open. In fact, that is why you do scenarios, so that you can put some frame around the endless possibilities in order not to drown in them. In the *application* phase, these futures you just created become given, fixed, set! You assume that the real future will unfold in the scenario space

---

20 Decisions are in the most basic sense ‚things you can do' or ‚choose not to do'. They depend on who you are (this is shorthand for your power, health, influence, charisma, debt, etc. etc.) - a prime minister can, and should, decide other things than a midwife can, on the time horizon you have chosen - choosing a university degree is different than planning your life, and on who you are with - a team can decide other things than an individual.

described by your four scenario stories and hope that as time goes by, you will be right.

From endless possibilities to four, from creativity to acceptance, from playful engagement to disciplined application - sounds like quite a damper, and believe me, it is. Given that we humans are not intrinsically good at changing perspectives at the drop of a hat, phase 7 is a challenge.

3 And finally, you can do the application in several different ways, depending on who you are and what your goals are.

Still, you have to do it. Without this phase, the entire scenario exercise will only result in ‚nice stories‘, but won‘t help you make better decisions.

Let us start by recalling explicitly where we are.

We have created a space of possible futures. These futures come alive through the four distinct plotlines (see graphic below).

The drivers are, as mentioned previously, the scaffolding we needed while constructing the scenario narratives. Once we have them – challenging,

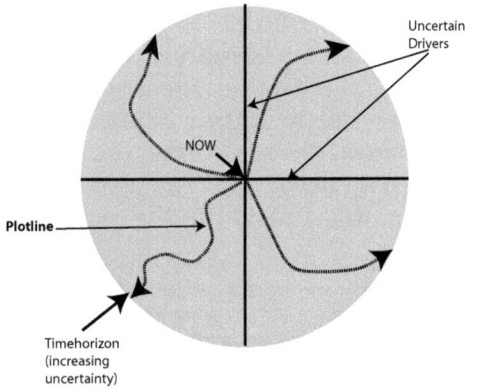

plausible, novel and consistent - we have compelling and memorable narratives. We can take the scaffolding away:

Now that the scenario narratives, or 'scenarios' for short, stand on their own and in their entirety

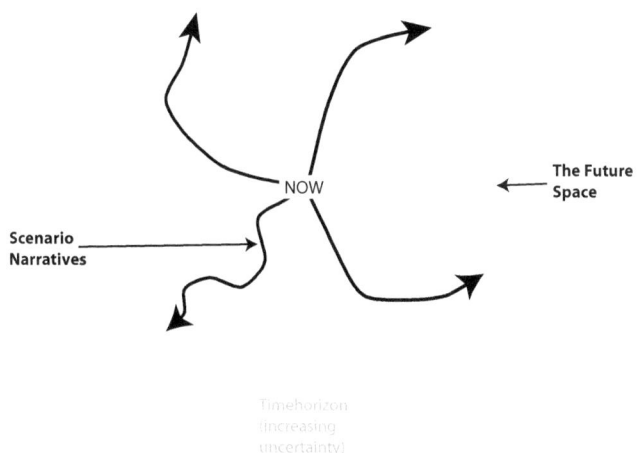

define the future space in relation to our driving question, we can **use** them.

You enter the picture

The first thing that happens is that **you** enter the picture. You and your role as individual, or family, or group (formal or ad-hoc), or department, or organization, or association, or NGO, etc. In other words, be very clear who the scenario user is and what role you are playing.

Second, you[21] must examine and answer two questions:

---

21 Remember, that you, your, me, etc. stands for you, the family, group, company, etc. that you decided on.

1) For **whose benefit** do you do want
   to use the scenarios, and

2) How much can **you influence** the future[22]?

The first question can be answered **primarily for 'yourself'** or **primarily for others**. The second question can be answered **hardly at all** or **quite a lot**[23]. Visually, you get the following picture:

You also need to be clear, especially when you do the application with more people than yourself,

For whose benefit?

	Primarily 'your' own	Primarily others
Hardly at all	*I*	*IV*
Quite a lot	*II*	*III*

How much can you influence the future?

what kind of benefit you have in mind. In compaies, benefit is usually financial, but even there it

---

22   The future as spanned by your four scenarios in relation to your driving question – NOT 'the future as such'. In other words, do not overload the scenarios with questions they were not created to shed light on.

23   Remember that life is analog. I.e. that the answers to the two questions lie on a continuum, they are NOT binary. The expressions – primarily for 'yourself', primarily for others, hardly at all and quite a lot – locate your answers on that continuum and thus make it easier to talk to others about them.

can be non-monetary like market share, clicks or growth (in volume, margin, cash-flow, etc.). In primarily non-economic organizations (like a family, an association, a band, a cooperative, etc.) the question of what kind of benefit you are after is quite diffuse. Spend time to clarify it at the start and agree amongst yourself!

Having reached answers to all the questions raised above (whose benefit, what kind, how much influence) you are finally ready to use the scenarios: select one of the four areas labeled with roman numerals, since the work to be done is different for each. What is confusing, as you will find out, is that there is some overlap in the steps of work, so keep a clear head!

Roman numeral I

Let us begin with the area roman numeral I – primarily your benefit, hardly any influence.

You move into the future by taking decisions in the here and now. Start with the ones you need to take anyway, with those that are pending and expand into the region of those you could take. Write them down and be as precise as possible. 'Fire employees' is not good enough – state whom, when, how and why you lay off people. Also make sure you write down decisions, not outcomes, to 'increase sales by 3%' is **not** a decision, it is an outcome.

Create a list of decisions

Create the list of decisions with the same people who will be responsible for implementing them later on. The more homogeneous the group, the easier the task is. The homogeneity can come from your

age, your field of study, your function in the organization, your interest, etc. The price you pay for
this ease, however, is that your range of the types of
decisions you come up with are often narrower than
if you have a few lateral thinkers, a few contrarians
in your group.

While writing down the decisions, note that they
are independent of the scenarios. They are decisions
you and / or your group can take in the here and
now. Obviously, they all should be within your, or
your group's, power to take. It serves no purpose to
contemplate decisions you have no power to take.

Draw the matrix

When you have written down all decisions, create a matrix that looks like the one on the opposite
page. The scenarios, i.e. the future space, are listed
horizontally at the top, your decisions are listed vertically on the left.

Fill in the matrix

Your next task is to fill in the matrix, call by cell
by cell, from D1 to Dn by answering the following
question for each individual decision: "If I take this
decision, how beneficial[24] will that be for 'me' in
scenario A, B, C or D?" Again, the 'me' is you, your
family, group, department, neighborhood association, etc.

You will have to go through each and every cell
of your matrix, from A1 all the way to Dn. For each
cell, you will reach a judgment in answer to the
benefit question above. Remember, scenarios have

---

24 Keeping in mind how you defined 'benefit' for you or your group earlier on.

If I take decision 1, how beneficial will that be for me, if scenario A comes true?

	Scenario **A**	Scenario **B**	Scenario **C**	Scenario **D**
Decision **1**	+ +	− −	+ +	+ +
Decision **2**	− −	−	−	+ +
Decision **3**	−	−	+	?
Decision **4**	?	+ +	− −	+
Decision **5**	− −	+	+ +	?
. . .	+	−	?	+
Decision **n**	+	+ +	+	+ +

a time horizon in them, so 'being beneficial' means throughout the unfolding of the particular scenario over time.

You should note the answers as either double positive (**++**), i.e. very beneficial, or simply positive (**+**), i.e. beneficial, neutral (**0** or **?**), i.e. not sure, simply negative (**−**) i.e. harmful, or doubly negative (**− −**), i.e. very harmful. You do this with each cell, one at a time, so budget some time for this, especially when you do this with others.

If you do work in a group, you can develop these judgments individually first and then compare your choices with the other participants in your group - and if you have come to different assessments, discuss / argue until you reach an agreement. Or you can discuss immediately every assessment with the whole group until a consensus is reached. The first mode of working takes longer but is often better.

When you are finished, your filled in matrix may look like this, but, of course, reflecting your judgments for each cell. Since I will refer back to this matrix later on, I call it **DM-B**, for decision matrix - benefit.

Analyze the decisions

Next, you analyze the decisions - horizontally, by row. If you look, for example, at *decision n*, the bottom one of your matrix, you'll notice that this decision is either 'beneficial' or 'very beneficial' for you in all possible scenarios. And remember, the four scenarios are to the best of your abilities your guess as to how the uncertain future will unfold, the space, in other words, in which reality, when it comes, will be situated. Hence, *decision n* is something you should take, since no matter how the future unfolds, this is a beneficial decision for you or 'your group'. A bit deprecatingly, these decisions are sometimes called 'no-brainers', but be sure to take them anyway, because they are beneficial for you!

More difficult is the analysis of the first row, *decision 1*. Taking that decision is 'really beneficial' in scenarios A, C, and D, but 'really harmful' for you in scenario B. Since you don't know which scenario will, in reality, unfold, you are left with a conundrum. What you need to do is more complicated than *decision n*, which you just took and then forgot about it. In the case of *decision 1*, you should take it, but do three additional things:

- first, set up a good monitoring system that tells you early enough if *scenario B* shows signs of becoming true, because if it does, you should reverse *decision 1* and get out,

- second, invest enough in an exit option for *decision 1* so that when it is time to move out, you can move fast,

- and third, manage your colleagues in such a way that they understand, that even though you are taking *decision 1*, you may be forced to revert this choice, namely when *scenario B* is that which is actually happening in real life.

It is this last point that in real life is the hardest to do right. Unless you are a real good manager of people, there is a great danger that you come across as weak, ambivalent and undecided, all character traits your fellow human beings rarely think very highly of. To me, however, people who can hold that tension are the true leaders of men and women.

Decision 2 presents the same conundrum, but with opposite signs. Here you most likely will not take the decision but invest enough to retain the 'right to play', should *scenario D* show convincing signs of coming true.

You continue the analysis with each decision, row by row. In the end, it will be much clearer to you what to do, what not to do, when to do it and how to do it. Thanks to scenarios - which allow you to test your decisions against a tableau of divergent, yet possible futures ahead of time - you are able to make better decisions today for an uncertain future tomorrow - the signal got stronger, and the noise receded.

Using scenarios in this manner is called **adapting to the future**. You may know it under the term 'contingency planning', 'risk mitigation' or 'risk management'. It is basically a **defensive** use of scenarios, done to maximize your benefit from your decisions when you have hardly any influence over the future.

To some, 'defensive risk management' may sound too dull and dreary. But don't dismiss it too lightly. If your influence on the future (as captured by your scenarios) is indeed limited, then that is all you can do. The limitation of influence does not have to be your fault – if, for example, your domain is the future of your family and your spouse just decided to leave, your influence on the future is limited. To have a plan B, and C and D may in this situation not be the worst thing. Similarly, if you are a start-up, you most likely find yourself here – roman numeral I.

Roman numeral II

This space is still primarily your benefit, but you have answered the question about influence with 'quite a lot'. Thus, you can do more than just react to the future, you can use the scenarios to shape the future to your benefit. Established organizations tend to be at this end of the influence continuum.

To be able to shape the future to your benefit, you need to step back and first decide which future, i.e. which scenario, you want to see come true.

Since you are using the scenarios primarily for your benefit, add up all the plusses and minuses in each scenario column vertically, using the previously created **DM-B**. The column with the highest score is the future that is the most beneficial to you. It is the one where all your decisions listed on the left, when seen as a portfolio of decisions, give the greatest benefit to you. In our example, this would be *scenario D*. There are only two decisions, 3 and 5, that would not be 'beneficial' for you or your group.

You could simply drop those decisions, i.e. not take them, or you could think of changing decisions

If I take decision 1, how beneficial will that be for me, if scenario A comes true?

	Scenario **A**	Scenario **B**	Scenario **C**	Scenario **D**
Decision **1**	+ +	− −	+ +	+ +
Decision **2**	− −	−	−	+ +
Decision **3**	−	−	+	?
Decision **4**	?	+ +	− −	+
Decision **5**	− −	+	+ +	?
. . .	+	−	?	+
Decision **n**	+	+ +	+	+ +

3 and 5 so that taking them would get you to at least a single plus, if not a double plus. But you leave, to begin with, the set of decisions largely intact. This is important, because decisions are usually tied to organizational structures, to resources, to careers and to egos, none of which you should underestimate and all of which are difficult to adjust.

Even though the selection is mechanic in the sense that you could assign a weighting to your assessments and sum by column[25], it is a way for you find the future that plays to your inherent strengths.

---

25 If ++ = 4, + = 3, ? = 2, − = 1 and − − = 0 then scenario A gets 13 points, B gets 14, C gets 17 and D gets 22

Having found the future that suits you best, you have, however, **no assurance** that this scenario, *scenario D* in our example, **actually will come true**. At worst, you could be preparing for a future that never comes true.

Hence, you need to embark now on a second part of the assessment, namely to pick decisions that make your preferred future, *scenario D*, more **likely**.

At the start of phase 7 you answered the question - How much can you influence the future? – with 'quite a lot'. Hence, you can redo the analysis cell by cell by cell, but, this time, asking a different question: If 'I', or 'we', were to take decision 1, would that make scenario A more or less likely in reality?

If I were to take decision 1, would that make scenario A more likely in reality?

	Scenario **A**	Scenario **B**	Scenario **C**	Scenario **D**
Decision **1**	—	— —	+ +	+
Decision **2**	—	+ +	—	— —
Decision **3**	+ +	+ +	+ +	+ +
Decision **4**	+	—	+ +	?
Decision **5**	—	?	?	+
. . .	+ +	— —	+	+
Decision **n**	+	+	?	— —

You start again with an empty matrix as before, scenarios across the top horizontally, the same decisions as before down the left, vertically. But now you make a **likelihood** judgment for each cell. You can use the same signs (**++**, **+**, **?**, **—** and **— —**) as before to signal much more likely, more likely, a wash-out, less likely, and much less likely. Be sure to use a different color from the first assessment, otherwise you can get quite confused about which matrix answered which question. If you do not see the plusses and minuses in blue on the previous page above, click on the link below the matrix to download it in color.

www.blue-way.net/shapeLikelyMatrixfilled.pdf

While *scenario D* is still 'our' preferred one - the result of the benefit assessment - when you make the likelihood judgment, the resulting matrix looks different - naturally, because you asked a different question. I call this likelihood matrix **DM-L**. In our example, *decisions 2* and *n*, which worked very positive for you during the first benefit assessment - **if** *scenario D* came true, turn out to make your preferred future actually much less likely.

What to do? Back to the drawing board, because you now need to make your set of decisions variable. What does that mean? You need to invent new decisions you can take whose purpose is twofold: *one*, taking them works out beneficial for you in your preferred scenario **and** *two*, it makes the preferred scenario more likely to come true.

Besides inventing new ones, you can also change existing ones, like *decision 2* and *n* in our example so that they do work out beneficial for you in your preferred scenario **and** make the preferred scenario more likely to come true. Alternatively, you can drop *decisions 2* and *n*.

What sounds like child's play, invent a decision, drop one, modify one, is excruciatingly difficult in real life. Because decisions are not free-floating figments of the imagination, they are connected to real people, real money, real hopes, real efforts and real hard work. You are messing with people's lives. All I can do is to urge you to do it with great respect, humility and understanding. If you don't, I can assure you, you won't get far with your future, preferred or not.

How many new decisions do you need? It depends on who is working on making any of the other scenarios come true. The bigger their arsenal, the more decisions you need to invent. And if at all possible, invent those that at the same time as they are making *your* future more likely, makes *theirs* much less likely. Killing two birds with one stone.

Using scenarios in this manner is called **shaping the future**. You may know it under the term 'pro-active planning', 'option generation' or 'tilting the playing field in your favor'. It is basically a **pro-active** use of scenarios, done to maximize your benefit from your decisions by using the influence you (believe you) have over the future to make the future that is most beneficial to you as likely as you possibly can in real life.

Roman numeral III

The technique of this usage is very similar to shaping the future (Roman Numeral II). But the difference is in its normative stance and its fundamental purpose. This is the scenario usage where you want to maximize the benefit NOT for *yourself* BUT for some *other*.

Consequently, you choose your preferred future from the point of view of 'a greater good'. This can be sustainable development goals, human rights, biodiversity, the best possible future for your children, or the like. In every case, this choice is moral, ethical and ideological, **not** driven by benefit accruing to you. Instead, the choice of your preferred future originates in a - often normative based - sense of how the future *should* be.

While normative based choices are often harder to arrive at, and much harder to convince others of their legitimacy, there is one great practical advantage in connection with scenarios, at least for the purists amongst you: you can skip the entire benefit consideration part (i.e. DM-B) because you have picked your preferred future on normative grounds. I said 'purist' because those are the ones who do not care about benefits at all. In real life the number of purists is limited, which is why you hear a lot about 'win-win' situations. You want to make your preferred future more likely, but at the same time, you do not want to scarifice too many of your benefits. For the champions of 'win-win' futures, you have no choice but to do the benefit analysis described earlier. (DM-B)

Either way, you need to rearrange, i.e. drop from, add to, modify, etc., your set of decisions to strengthen the chances in real life that your preferred future scenario will come true - i.e. you want to increase the *likelihood* of your normatively chosen scenario to come true. The technique for doing that is detailed in 'Roman numeral II (DM-L) above.

Using scenarios in this manner is called **trans-forming the future**. You may know it under the term 'deep change', 'transformative innovation' or the like. It is again a **pro-active** use of scenarios, but done to maximize the benefit of some other (humanity, your neighborhood, the ones who cannot speak for themselves, etc.) from decisions you take by using the influence you (believe you) have over the future to make the preferred future as likely as you possible can in real life. Foundations, social enterprises and NGOs often operate here.

When embarking on this use of scenarios be sure to speak to the ones, on whose behalf you claim to transform the future into a better one, beforehand.

Roman numeral IV

This is the scenario usage where you want to maximize the benefit NOT for yourself BUT for some other, AND you have hardly any influence over the future.

When trying to imagine this use of scenarios in practical terms I was hard pressed to come up with a situation that corresponds to maximizing benefits for others and no influence. Until I thought of family situations. When you make decisions about the future of your children, or the choice of an old-age home for your parents, you find yourself in this difficult spot. On a larger scale, when trying to re-build a country after a civil war, you also most likely find yourself in this situation. Mentoring and teaching would, in my opinion, also qualify.

The technique for working in this area is that you do the benefit analysis of roman numeral I (adapting to the future – DM-B) but with the added twist that it is not **your** benefit you evaluate in all scenarios, but that of the third party. Very difficult, but highly rewarding when you get it right.

For using scenarios in this manner there is no common name, at least not one I am aware of. Perhaps, one could call it **giving someone else a head start**. If you know of better terms, let me know. It is a **defensive** use of scenarios, done to maximize the benefit of some other (your children, your neighborhood, your parents, etc.) from decisions you take 'for them' when you have hardly any influence over the(ir) future.

Once more, when embarking on this use of scenarios be sure to speak to the ones, on whose behalf you make decision for them, beforehand.

Communicating

Besides doing your assessment, you should communicate your scenario narratives as part of your application work. Doing so lets you:

- talk to those who normally shun you: scenarios allow the engagement of outsiders in constructive conversations that they would otherwise not participate in. Why? Because one is dealing with the still wide-open future, rather than arguing about the present.

- get everyone on the same page: scenarios are one of the better mechanisms to align stakeholders with different perspectives on the same subject towards a common purpose.

- frame the conversation.

When using scenarios to try to transform the future (Roman Numeral III), communicating the scenarios becomes almost as important as creating them in first place. Transformative scenarios almost always aim to reframe an issue, a problem or an intractable dilemma. Reframing is another word for getting people to see things from a different perspective, and that is one of the hardest things to do respectfully, yet successfully.

Next step

Once you have your robust and thoroughly tested set of decisions get them properly implemented with all the effort, diligence and follow-up necessary.

During implementation, learn from what you are doing, especially your mistakes, so that next time, at the very least you won't be repeating mistakes you've made in the past. This can be as informal as regular self-reflection by you and your implementation team or go all the way to formal action research that observes, as objectively as possible, what you are doing and draws generalized lessons from it.

With the application of scenarios, you rejoin the majority of humanity. Most of whom, however, will have jumped in right here, without much thought or deliberation. If you don't know where you are going, all roads will lead you astray - as the saying goes.

So next time you have to take decisions about something that matters, consider a scenario exercise, large or small, involving lots of people or few, being costly or not, before you make your commitments. In the medium to long term, it will save you time and energy, make you more effective and prepare you for unknown futures.

EPILOGUE
SCENARIOS ARE ABOUT PEOPLE AND THE FUTURE

This book is meant to be a practical ‚how-to' guide. Still, even if you follow all the advice of this little book very closely, you may find that a particular scenario exercise does not work out the way you wanted it to. This has happened to me several times in my life as a scenario facilitator and the only common thread among the failed projects was that key people I worked with did not really like people.

At first, this seemed an odd conclusion to me, but the more I reflect on this, the more I've come to realize that scenarios allow and invite you to pay real attention to others, to listen empathetically, to put yourself in the shoes of someone else, to serve and respect others and to help ordinary people reach for the stars. If this kind of intimacy makes you uncomfortable, then perhaps scenarios are not for you. Perhaps, instead, you can serve humanity better by getting a job developing the next great algorithm.

Second, remind yourself repeatedly that the future is completely ahead of you and all others. Even though you will spend the rest of your life in the future, no one has ever been there, and no one ever will. No one knows what it will look, feel, smell and taste like. I personally think this is a good thing. It makes the future subject to my influencing it and gives me great serenity.

So, approach the future with humility, be skeptical of people who claim to know what will happen and remain open to surprises, wonder, even magic.

Because life is not the sum of the days you will have counted at the end, instead it is all about the days, and the moments, that truly count.

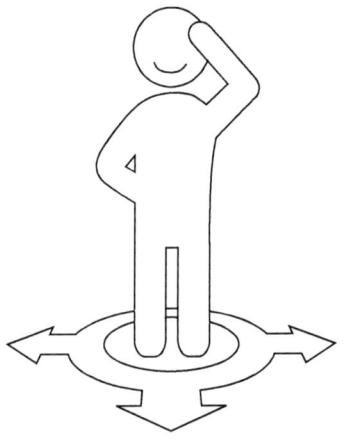

APPENDIX: PRACTICALITIES

Core team

The size and composition of a core team are often a question of your budget. For a full-fledged exercise, you need about nine months of time and about 250,000 Euros. Big ticket items are the time of the core team and the residential workshops with about 40% each. If you get them sponsored, directly or in-kind, so much the better.

Ideally, you work with:

- a project director, who leads the team, is an experienced facilitator and interviewer and can run projects on time and on budget. He or she is the plenary facilitator.

- four small group facilitators

- a writer / editor

- one or two researchers

- an organizational wizard, who is responsible for the logistics of everything, i.e. organizing the interviews, the meetings of the core team as well as the workshops, oversees the production and keeps everybody on their toes. This person is also the controller of the finances and the liaison to the funder(s).

Plenary and small group facilitation can be switched, and in my mind actually should be switched, so that significant learning also takes place within the core team itself.

Writer

The role of the writer is separate because that person's responsibility is to serve the group. While it is true that everybody in the core team's role is to serve the group of participants, everybody but the writer also has the obligation to drive, to motivate and to encourage the participants to deliver their absolutely best that they are able to give. Thus, it is the writer who becomes the voice, the advocate of the participants in the work of the core team (and the overall process).

Growing the team, veto

Assemble a team you really like to work with, open, playful, yet disciplined and reliable, where each member can blindly rely on the others when needed. And trust me, during the course of a scenario exercise, each of you will need the others. Blind trust at the extreme means that as you grow your team, each member already part of the team has an unconditional veto on who joins. And during discussions.

'Unconditional' means in this context a veto where no one has to give reasons for their veto. What happens if two opposite vetoes are exercised by two people at the same time? If the team is really strong, then members accept the 'verdict' without really understanding why it was exercised and use the resulting tension to go even deeper in their comprehension, knowledge, and grasp of the issue. Unfortunately, in not-so-strong teams, this kind of situation may lead to separation - not really a morale booster, and certainly an organizational calamity.

To minimize the chances for this kind of worst case, try to stay away from people with egos so big that can't fit through a door, from the ones who know, from the ones who always have to be right, from the ones who always need to be center-stage and the ones who hold a grudge against people. They take energy away from you, the team and even the participants.

Be a mentor

Involve in each exercise one or two people who fit the description above, but lack the experience. Scenario planning is learned by doing, from mentors. Share what you know. It's a little bit like swimming. You can watch all the video clips of great swimmers, learn all about buoyancy, lung capacity, rhythm to breathe - but in the end, you got to jump in. Help others take the plunge.

Basic knowledge of the process

To make your life easier, make sure one or two team members in addition to you have done a complete scenario exercise before - preferably with you. Otherwise you need to set aside time to run them through a mock exercise which lasts two full days. They should have read about scenarios processes beforehand - from this book, or another one you may run across and prefer. If you skip this, you'll end up having to interrupt repeatedly the real work of planning and delivering the project for the participants. At the least, this creates disturbances in the rhythm of the work, it drains energy unnecessarily and in a worst case leads to frustration and (strong) irritation.

Starting a project

Unfortunately, all of these issues pop up most intensely during the most difficult phase of any project, namely the change from a brilliant thought to a team with money but real personalities and constraints and a job to do. So when you do your planning, double the time and resources you thought you'd needed for this part. Also, take a deep breath, do the best you can with patience, modesty and empathy - but **do** it! Otherwise your project will simply be another one in the long line of exercises in sustainable talking. In American English there is a, slightly rude, saying for this: Shit, or get off the pot.

Scenario projects are like making a movie

Organizationally, scenario work has much in common with movie making. You come temporarily together to create something remarkable and memorable, work very intensely with each other during that time, celebrate the success and disband again. There is no safety net, no job to go back to and no one to comfort you when the project turns out to have been a disaster. But there *is* creativity, next to no bureaucratic constraints (save for the due diligence with the money the project has been entrusted with) and, above all, the chance to work directly on something meaningful for a while. In today's reality of a locus of control over what you are supposed to do far, far removed, of the relentless quest to cut costs again and again and again, and of having to sell yourself with marketing phrases devoid of any meaning, scenario projects are an opportunity to taste real life again, even if for just a little while. Savor the experience.

What is a great facilitator?

A good leader is someone the people love. A bad leader is someone the people hate. But a truly great leader is one where the people say: We did it ourselves. Replace 'leader' with 'facilitator', and then you have it.

Facilitators should have these skills:

- neutrality - without having no opinion

- professionalism - without the arrogance of those who know

- empathy - without denying their own identity

- trustworthiness - without betraying the trust that is given to them

- patience - without losing sight of the goal

A facilitator is *not* a moderator, even though these words are sometimes used interchangeably. Moderators dampen, calm down and dissipate energy out of, at times, heated discussions. A facilitator injects energy into a group, to encourage them to go beyond where each member of the group would dare to go on their own.

Do you really need all these interviews, workshops and core team people?

Nine months and 250,000 Euros can seem like a lot of time and money. So, can do with less? The answer is yes, but.

To go the other extreme, let me mention to you that several high school teachers in the area of Aachen, Germany have been using scenarios with their students as part of their normal classroom teaching. With no extra money, about 12 school hours and enthusiastic students.

I also give three-day workshops in which I teach people the why and how of scenarios. The days consist of some theory, but mostly of a simulation of the entire process, i.e. all the seven phases including the last application phase. Though 'just' a simulation, it still creates deep conversation, debate and deliberation of possible futures and how to get there.

So what do nine months and oodles of money add that you don't get in three days? In a word, you get *resilience*: if you work with many interviewees, workshop participants and a professional core team, the emerging scenario stories are more robust. Just like two heads are better than one, the added perspectives let you explore, consider and investigate many more possibilities than doing it alone, or with just a handful of people. This is absolutely critical in two situations:

- when reframing an issue for a large group of people, even a whole society
- when your decisions involve a lot, and I do mean a lot, of resources.

The reframing is in my mind the harder one. Because most people are not aware that the way they think about an issue is but one of many possible. For most of us, a frame isn't really a frame; it is the TRUTH. ‚Reframing' is touching the innermost core of our beliefs, that's why it is so difficult. So the very least, I submit, is for you to have done your homework properly, checked it three times over and do it as accurately as possible - before you ‚invite' others to a new way of looking at their world. A new way of seeing inevitably leads to new ways of acting. Be careful what you set in motion.

Big resource commitments are easier to support with scenario planning because intuitively we understand that this is part of, maybe unusual, but required risk management. And the mental models of how to manage risk can relatively easily accommodate scenarios. Still, the higher the stakes, the better your work must be.

The reason why 12 hours in a school setting work is twofold:

- for most students it is just one more method they have to learn, they rarely get emotionally involved. A bit like learning the multiplication tables, though the feedback we get is that it is much more fun than that

- when they do get emotionally involved it is usually when they are asked to develop scenarios about jobs in the future. For a teenager, this matters.

If you are a teacher, or a student, and are interested in using scenarios in your classroom, have a look at our site[26] that will help you further. It is completely free, but so far only available in German.

Confidentiality - a safe space for work

Scenario work has the tendency of cutting to the chase, of getting relentlessly to the point. While scenario work is group work, you do get close to an individual's beliefs, dreams, hopes, and fears. You find out what really matters to them. Such intimacy

---

26 http://www.szenarien-in-schulen.net/

is rare in professional work, and even in a private setting can easily be misused. It is your and your core team's responsibility to make *absolutely* sure that the abuse of that intimacy never ever happens. So a big part of your work is to create, maintain and defend a safe space for the work. In today's world of twitter and smart phones a real challenge. The only way I've been able to deliver on the promise of confidentiality is through trust.

Cascade of Trust

Trust, however, is a funny bird. You can't buy it, you can't store it, you can't even make someone trust you. All you can do is to behave in a trustworthy manner. That is, be worthy of someone else's trust in you. Whether or not they then choose to confer trust on you is again beyond your influence. Tricky stuff - which is probably why throughout history people relied more on coercion, and worse, in their dealings with each other.

To make matters worse, you may work with people who have never experienced themselves this bond of unconditional trust with anyone. In German, we have a word for that - Urvertrauen - which is clumsily translated to English as "sense of basic trust. What infants are learning … is a "sense of basic trust" (or mistrust) in the world. If their needs are met promptly and lovingly, they come to feel that the world is a benign place, a place where good things generally happen and bad experiences are soon rectified."[27]

---

27 http://dict.leo.org/forum/viewUnsolvedquery.php?idThread=165832&idForum=1&lang=de&lp=ende

Still, it is worth the effort, because in a trusting environment, creativity, courage, and respect do flow and build upon on each other; and are all necessary ingredients for powerful scenarios to emerge.

So, you and your team start by behaving worthy of the interviewees' and workshop participants' trust. You make it clear to the interviewees that on top of the information they give you, you also ask them to *entrust* this information through you to the first workshop, in which a handful of interviewees should participate to act a bit like guardians of that trust.

Similarly, the participants of the first workshop also *entrust* their work, their deliberations and their struggles to you and your team to make sure it flourishes in the second workshop. Again, a few participants of the first should be in the second workshop - as bearers of knowledge *and* as guardians of that trust.

Finally, the last workshop *entrusts* all that has been done so far to the writer (who must be present during both workshops so people can make a judgment if he or she is indeed worthy of their trust).

I've been in processes where the last hand-over did not work and I am sorry to say, all the work was in vain.

You know you did your job well is when interviewees and workshop participants say upon reading the scenario stories: 'If I knew how to write, this is exactly what I would have liked to have written'. A grammatically convoluted praise, but the highest praise your team can get.

If this all sounds a bit esoteric to you, a very good place to start is to say what you do and to do what you say. Sounds almost too simple, but isn't. Live it!

Flow of energy

Be prepared to inject a lot of energy into the process in the beginning and during the workshops. Why? Because people are asked to step outside their 'comfort zone'. While this is exhilarating, especially in a safe space, it becomes at times overwhelming. The natural response when you are overwhelmed is to retreat to familiar ground. To hold participants 'on this edge' requires sensitivity, reassurance, and energy. Which all come primarily from you and your team. It is towards the end of the process, when the emerging stories change from being figments of the imagination to real frames for the future, that all the energy you put in flows back to you. You will feel it most strongly at the event, the celebration when you release the stories into the public world. Forgive me the analogy, but it all is a bit like giving birth.

Difficult participant / team member

One of Dilbert's Principles[28] is that in every group there is at least one person you should dismiss. Unfortunately, on rare occasions, this very person is in your project.

How to recognize them?

- They are people who need to be right, and, one level of additional pain, they need you to admit publicly that you are wrong.

---

28 Scott Adams, 1996, *The Dilbert principle: a cubicle's-eye view of bosses, meetings, management fads & other workplace afflictions*, New York, HarperBusiness ISBN 978-0887308581

- They prove to you, usually in a plenary, that your methodology is flawed, unscientific, too scientific, etc., in short, useless for the task.

- They prove to you, again usually in the plenary, that someone else, usually a dark power, has already decided on the outcome and uses this process as a shabby charade to simulate legitimacy.

- They are unable or unwilling to suspend disbelief and or to change perspectives - and try to impose this attitude on the entire process. They know.

- They are on a mission, and men (or women) on a mission tend to subject everything to the task of fulfilling that mission. Even scenario processes, where they use participants, ideas and the process itself to get their missionary job done.

- They are ‚reasonable‘. By this, I mean the following. Especially during the opening, the creative phases of the process when people are learning to fly the resonable people quietly sit back and watch and listen. As the euphoria levels off when people are all of the sudden realizing that they just flew, the reasonable people will clear their throat and say in a low voice: „I fully agree with what has been said so far, and I really like the creativity we just witnessed" - then they hold their breath for a few more seconds before they go one - "**but**, we are all reasonable people here in this room, and I am afraid we all know that what you are talking about is, unfortunately, just not possible in the real world."

Then he or she sits down again. When this happens, you literally feel the energy dissipating in a second. The room just crashed. The people who just flew get visibly smaller and are often ashamed that as reasonable people they foolishly dared to spread their wings.

- I am sure you can add your own examples.

If he or she is in your core team, it is deadly. You may go through the motions of running the process, but you may as well not have bothered. Unless you can dismiss the person, at least from the team, or give him or her another task in the organization, it is over. This is the worst case.

If you meet someone like that during an interview, it is a squandered interview, but the damage is limited. Unless that person takes his or her criticism public and gets attention. My personal experience is that they rarely do get the public's attention because they are known to be 'difficult' and your project is just another random example of their disdain.

If you have someone like that in a workshop, do not expose him or her in front of others. Instead, you or one of your team should seek a private conversation, paying close attention to the critical behavior. In most cases, we have been able to deflect the criticism by appealing to the right of the other participants to have a productive workshop and second, by actually agreeing to visit him or her outside the workshop - could be their work place, or some neutral ground - and taking the time to understand the motivation of their behavior. Surprisingly often, this is very helpful for both parties. The outcome of such meetings has in my experience been twofold:

- The person agrees to withdraw from the project, but not in anger.

- The person agrees to accept the rules of the workshop and reframes it as a, often personal, learning experience, even though his or her skepticism is not diminished. In this latter case, it often helps to give this person a public and official critical role, for example as fact checker, as plausibility inspector or the like.

A Scenario *Process* is not Public

I mentioned several times the confidentiality of the interviews and the work in the workshops. The logical consequence is that the entire process is not public. You must create, maintain and defend the safe space in which participants work hard so that powerful scenarios can emerge. Unless the space is safe, they may well think the unthinkable, question the obvious and challenge the official future, but they are not going to tell you, or anybody else for that matter, anything about it. The work will bubble along the surface, voicing officially sanctioned platitudes and leading to scenarios, that are, well, nice. But without impact, without zest, without challenge, without life.

So, keep the cameras away, do your communication about the process very low key, no splashy infographics or flyers, keep expectations low. And absolutely no communication about the content. Until the scenario-stories are done. Then, and only then, give the *stories* a real hand for a good start in their life.

THE END

... and thanks for your attention!